Foreword

Owning guinea pigs can be incredibly rewarding and a great source of companionship. Pets can provide opportunities for social interactions, helping people feel less lonely and isolated. Growing up with pets also offers health benefits, and caring for an animal can help improve a child's social skills, encouraging the development of compassion, understanding and a respect for living things. Having guinea pigs is, however, a huge responsibility and requires long-term commitment in terms of care and finances.

Before getting guinea pigs, it is important that time is taken to discuss the commitment and care required with all family members, and that everyone agrees to having and looking after guinea pigs. Bear in mind that once you have your guinea pigs there is a legal requirement under the Animal Welfare Act 2006 to care for them properly, so you must be sure that you will be able to do this throughout your guinea pigs' life. This means providing somewhere suitable for them to live, a healthy diet, opportunities to behave normally, the provision of appropriate company, and ensuring that they are well.

If you are able to care for guinea pigs properly and make the decision to go ahead, then please consider giving a home to some of the many guinea pigs currently in the RSPCA's animal centres throughout England and Wales.

This book is based on up-to-date knowledge of guinea pig behaviour and welfare approved by the RSPCA. It has been written to provide you with all the care information you need to keep your guinea pigs happy and healthy throughout your lives together. We hope you enjoy it.

Samantha Gaines BSc (Hons) MSc PhD
Alice Potter BSc (Hons) MSc
Lisa Richards BSc (Hons)
Jane Tyson BSc (Hons) MSc PhD
Animal behaviour and welfare experts, Companion
Animals Department, RSPCA

Introduction

Owning and caring for a pair or group of guinea pigs can be great fun and very rewarding. But it is also a long-term commitment and a big responsibility in terms of care and cost. Typically, guinea pigs live for 5–6 years, but some may live longer, so you will need to think carefully about lots of different things to decide whether you are able to give them the care and attention they need over their lifetimes. Here are some of the things you need to consider:

Does keeping pets fit in with your lifestyle?

Although traditionally they are thought of as good first pets for children, guinea pigs have complex needs that must be met if they are to stay happy and healthy, so an adult should always be responsible for ensuring the guinea pigs are properly handled and cared for every day. Think very carefully about whether keeping guinea pigs fits in with your lifestyle. You will need to make sure that you can meet all their welfare needs, which includes feeding them every day, spending time grooming them and keeping their home clean, as well as interacting with them on a daily basis.

Guinea pigs are a long-term commitment

Typically, guinea pigs live for around 5–6 years, although some may live longer. Think very carefully about whether you can afford the cost of caring for guinea pigs over that period of time. Some of the things you will need to consider are the cost of a suitably robust home for them, food and bedding, equipment, vet bills and insurance. There may also be additional costs if you need to pay for boarding them whenever you are away. Remember that guinea pigs should be kept as pairs or in a group, so you must ensure that you have enough time to look after them all and meet their individual needs. You should also factor in the increased costs involved in keeping multiple pets, such as the possibility that they may need veterinary treatment at the same time, which can be expensive.

Guinea pigs are sociable, 'chatty' animals

This means that they must be kept with at least one other friendly guinea pig, unless a vet or suitable behaviour expert has advised you otherwise. A good mix is a male that has been neutered and one or more females, or a single-sex pair from the same litter. Female littermates usually live happily together, but male littermates may still fight. Guinea pigs should not be kept with other animals, including rabbits.

Guinea pigs are active, inquisitive animals

They need a home that provides plenty of space to run around and mental stimulation to stop them getting bored. It must include hiding places, somewhere to sleep and rest, toys and enough room for them to stretch out fully when lying down in any direction. A traditional hutch will not meet all their needs, so you must make sure you have enough space for a suitable shelter with permanent access to an exercise area.

The Animal Welfare Act

Under the Animal Welfare Act 2006, animal owners have a legal obligation to care for their animals properly by meeting five welfare needs. These are: a suitable place to live, a healthy diet including clean, fresh water, the ability to behave normally, appropriate company and protection from pain, suffering, injury and illness. This care guide contains lots of information and tips to help you make sure these needs are met.

LIFE HISTORY

SCIENTIFIC NAME *Cavia aperea f. porcellus*

GESTATION PERIOD 63 days (approx.)

NAME OF YOUNG Pups

LITTER SIZE Varies between 1 and 6; 3–4 is usual (approx.)

EYES OPEN At birth

WEANING AGE 14–21 days

PUBERTY Varies with sex, size and type of guinea pig; 2–4 months (approx.)

ADULT WEIGHT Varies greatly, can be up to 1.2kg (2.6lbs) (approx.)

LIFE EXPECTANCY Average of 5–6 years, up to 8 years possible (approx.)

Choosing the right type of guinea pig for you

If you are certain that you will be able to care for guinea pigs, the next stage is to do plenty of research to decide which type of guinea pig is right for you. If you are uncertain about anything to do with guinea pigs or their care, before or after you get your pets, remember that you can always seek expert advice from your vet, a suitable behaviour expert or rehoming organization that specializes in guinea pigs – see page 47 for more details.

Age

If you have decided that baby guinea pigs, or pups, are suitable for your family and lifestyle, you will need to make sure that, as well as being happy and healthy, they have been weaned and are ready to leave their mother. Weaning is usually complete by around 3 weeks, but baby guinea pigs should be at least 4 weeks old before leaving their mother so that they have had time to learn from her about feeding and to become confident and stronger.

Sex

Personal taste apart, there is little significance in the choice between male and female guinea pigs. If you are keeping mixed sexes, it is advisable to have males neutered to minimize the risk of unwanted pregnancies – neutering is uncommon for females as it is a complicated procedure. Speak to your vet for detailed advice about neutering and when to do it.

Size

Guinea pigs vary in size and shape, but all of them need plenty of space to run about in. If you are choosing from a litter of pups, it is easy to overlook how big the guinea pigs may get, but it is important to remember that, as they should be kept in pairs or a group, they will need a spacious home. Think very carefully, therefore, about whether you will have the space they need to be happy and healthy. A general guide to types of guinea pig, with examples, can be found on the next page.

Health

Whatever type of guinea pig you're thinking of getting, it's important to find out what health, behaviour and physical issues they may be prone to developing. As well as causing pain and suffering to your guinea pigs, this may also mean expensive bills for veterinary treatment and it may be more difficult to keep them happy and healthy. Knowing which types of guinea pig tend to have fewer problems will give you the best chance of getting happy, healthy pets.

Take time to select the right guinea pigs. Doing lots of research before you buy will help you to pick healthy animals.

Types of guinea pig

Guinea pigs originated in South America and it is thought that they were first domesticated several thousand years ago. There are many varieties of guinea pig, or 'cavies' as they are sometimes called. Three standard breeds were originally recognized: the English, which has a smooth, short coat; the Abyssinian, which has a rosetted or rough coat; and the long-haired Peruvian. Many more breeds and varieties now exist, and you will find guinea pigs with different-coloured coats and types of fur.

Some people may like a particular type of guinea pig because of their looks. Keep in mind, however, that you need to look beyond these generalizations, as every guinea pig has their own unique character and temperament. The way they behave will depend upon how they are reared, cared for and treated.

Coat and colours

Guinea pigs have different coat types: smooth, satin, rough, long or hairless. They also have hair in many different coat colours, including white, red, tan, brown, chocolate, cream, golden beige, lilac and black. Some guinea pigs, called 'bi-colours', have coats in blocks of two colours. Guinea pigs with coats in three blocks of colour are known as 'tri-colours'. Some have patterns, such as the Dalmatian, with its white coat and black spots. The Himalayan has white fur, with black or brown ears, nose and feet.

Smooth-haired

Smooth-haired guinea pigs have short, smooth, straight hair. Smooth-haired guinea pigs that are a single colour are called 'selfs'. Some smooth-haired guinea pigs have bi- or tri-coloured coats. Varieties of smooth-haired guinea pigs include the English or American.

✅ TOP TIP

Whatever type of guinea pigs you choose, remember that they should not be kept with other animals, including rabbits, because their needs and diet are completely different.

Rough-haired

These varieties include the Abyssinian, which has short, coarse hair in whorls or rosettes. Rex guinea pigs tend to have shorter coats with dense, rough fur – they look quite similar to the Teddy, which has short, coarse, thick hair, but Rexes tend to have crinkled whiskers, whereas the Teddy's whiskers are usually straight.

Long-haired

Peruvian guinea pigs have fine hair that grows very long and if it is not trimmed will trail on the ground. This may not be obvious when they are babies, so it is an easy thing to overlook when you are buying your pets. The Texel guinea pig has long hair in ringlets and curls all over the body that is very thick and needs particularly careful grooming. Long-haired guinea pigs are probably not the best choice for inexperienced owners or those with very busy lifestyles, because while all guinea pigs need regular grooming, those with long-haired coats need considerably more care and attention and it can be very difficult to tell the condition of the guinea pig underneath all the hair.

Hairless

The Baldwin guinea pig is born with hair but becomes totally bald at the time of weaning. The Skinny pig is hairless except for the head and lower legs. These guinea pigs are susceptible to the cold and also at risk of sunburn, so are not recommended for inexperienced owners.

LEFT TO RIGHT: English; Abyssinian; Peruvian; Hairless.

LEFT: Make sure that your new guinea pigs are healthy. ABOVE: There are many guinea pigs waiting to be rehomed at RSPCA animal centres.

Getting guinea pigs

Where to buy

You may have decided what size, sex and type of guinea pig is most suitable for your family, but you should then take your time in selecting the right pets.

The RSPCA encourages anyone looking for guinea pigs to consider taking on some of the thousands of animals it rescues each year. Rehoming charities often have guinea pigs of all different types and colours looking for a good home, some of which will be bonded pairs or groups. Alternatively, they may be able to pair suitable guinea pigs for you.

If you are planning to buy your guinea pigs directly from the person who bred them, do some research first to make sure you choose a responsible breeder. Breeders should be happy to discuss with you subjects such as how the guinea pigs have been kept, and should invite you to visit their home. This is important because you should try to see the baby guinea pigs (pups) with their mothers as this will give you a good picture of how well they have been cared for, and seeing the parent will give you a fair indication of the guinea pigs' eventual size and sociability.

If you are going to buy a guinea pig from a pet shop, only buy from an outlet that meets all the welfare needs of the animals in its care and also ensures that this information is freely available for potential owners.

Meeting your guinea pigs

Whether you are buying your guinea pigs from a rehoming centre, breeder or a pet shop, it is a good idea to call or visit first. The person you are getting your guinea pigs from should be happy to talk to you and answer any questions you may have. When you visit, look for signs that the litter (and parents) seem healthy and well cared for. If you feel that anything is not quite right about the situation, it may be best to walk away and choose your guinea pigs from somewhere else.

Information

When you get your guinea pigs you should be supplied with information to help you care for them. This should include a care sheet telling you how they have been looked after so far. It is particularly important to find out about the guinea pigs' diet and what types of food they are used to. Ideally you should be given a week's food for each guinea pig, too, as any sudden changes to their diet could make them ill.

Finding healthy guinea pigs

Wherever you view your guinea pigs, you should always check that they are healthy. Here are some signs that may indicate that a guinea pig has an underlying medical problem:

- Being under- or overweight
- Lethargy or lack of interest in surroundings
- Weakness, wobbliness or difficulty standing up
- Difficulty walking, or not using a limb
- Noisy, rapid, shallow or laboured breathing
- A dirty coat that is tangled or matted
- Hair loss or scratching (could be signs of parasites such as mites)
- Wounds or sores on the skin, legs or feet
- Discharge or inflammation in the ears
- Discharge from the nose or eyes
- Signs of discomfort or pain when urinating, such as squealing in distress
- Staining, sores or signs of diarrhoea around the tail or bottom, including dirty or matted fur
- Overgrown, dirty, uneven or misaligned teeth
- Not eating or difficulty eating
- A wet chin or drooling
- Overgrown or damaged claws

These are just a few examples. If you notice anything at all that does not look quite right with the guinea pigs you have seen, you may want to consider getting your pet from somewhere else. If you have concerns about the welfare of any of the animals you have visited, call the RSPCA (details can be found at www.rspca.org.uk).

LEFT: When buying from a breeder, try to see baby guinea pigs with their mother.

Biology

Rodents

Guinea pigs belong to the rodent family, which includes other animals that are kept as pets such as rats, mice, gerbils and hamsters. In the wild, rodents include squirrels, dormice and capybaras. The feature that all rodents have in common is their teeth, which are especially adapted for gnawing. In fact, the word rodent comes from the Latin word 'rodere', which means 'to gnaw'.

Exaggerated features

Some varieties of guinea pig have been bred to emphasize certain physical features, which over time have become more exaggerated. For example, some breeds have very long fur, which may get tangled and matted, causing suffering and reducing their quality of life. Others have been bred to have no fur or to lose their hair shortly after birth, which means they are very vulnerable to changes in temperature and must live indoors. Some of these issues will result in lifelong health problems and suffering, so try to ensure that

any guinea pigs you choose are free from exaggerated features.

Teeth

A guinea pig's top front teeth are called 'incisors'. They grow continuously and very quickly, which is why guinea pigs need to gnaw to help wear them down. Eating plenty of grass and hay helps them to do this, but they also need a gnawing block made from untreated wood to keep their teeth healthy. It is important to check their teeth regularly. If you notice any problems, such as difficulty eating, not eating, a wet chin or drooling, seek veterinary advice immediately.

Digestion

Guinea pigs have an unusual way of digesting food. It passes through the gut and emerges as soft droppings called 'caecotrophs'. These are eaten, directly from their bottom, which allows the food to be reingested. Caecotrophs are dietary essentials for a guinea pig to get all of the nutrients they need before any waste matter is passed as hard, pellet-like droppings.

Babies

The average guinea pig pregnancy lasts for around 63 days, which is a relatively long time. Newborn guinea pigs, or pups, have a fully-furred coat, can walk around and already have their eyes and ears open.

Claws

A guinea pig's claws grow constantly. Usually their claws will wear down as they move, especially if they move across a floor which is solid, such as concrete, but they should be checked regularly to make sure they are not damaged or overgrown.

If your guinea pigs' claws need trimming, it is best to get this done by a vet or other pet-care expert. (See page 38 for more on health and welfare.)

Eyes

Guinea pigs have bright, beady eyes. Some guinea pigs have red eyes because of a lack of pigment cells; they are known as 'albinos'.

Vitamin C

Like humans, guinea pigs cannot make vitamin C, nor can they store it for long periods. This means that guinea pigs must have vitamin C in their diet from sources such as leafy greens and guinea pig nuggets, otherwise they could become very ill. For more information about making sure your guinea pigs get enough vitamin C, see page 41.

Environment

1

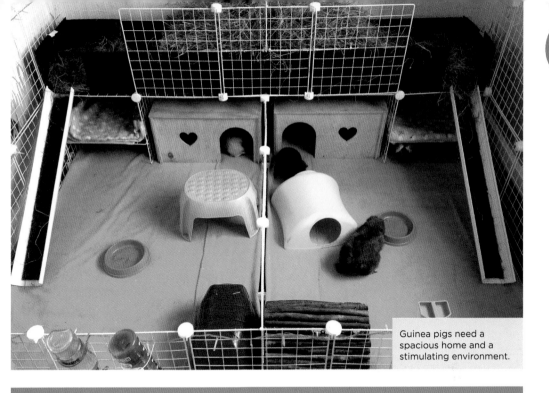

Guinea pigs need a spacious home and a stimulating environment.

A suitable place to live

Before you bring your guinea pigs home, make sure you have prepared a suitable, secure, hazard-free place for them to live and that you have everything they will need to be happy and well looked after. Here are some things to consider:

A home, not a hutch

Guinea pigs are active animals. A traditional small hutch will not give them the space and stimulating environment that they need in order to live a happy and healthy life. Keeping guinea pigs in a small hutch can cause health and behaviour problems.

Guinea pigs need to live in a space that has a shelter for sleeping, resting and hiding, and permanent access to somewhere that is big enough for each of them to explore, run, play, hide and stretch out fully in any direction. They also need to be able to stand up fully on their back legs. For more information on suitable homes, see www.rspca.org.uk/guinea pigs/environment.

A shelter and living enclosure

Your guinea pigs' home should have two areas; a main shelter and a living enclosure. The main shelter consists of an enclosed, darkened area with solid walls and roof for sleeping, resting and hiding. It must be large enough for all the guinea pigs to rest together comfortably. ▶

LEFT: Make sure your guinea pigs have daily access to their enclosure if it is not permanently attached to their shelter. ABOVE: Guinea pigs should be housed in a quiet, calm place. RIGHT: Some people prefer to keep their guinea pigs indoors.

Wherever possible, this should be integrated and permanently attached to a large living enclosure such as an exercise run, which should allow your guinea pigs to see out. Your guinea pigs' outdoor living enclosure or run must have a secure roof made from wire mesh to prevent predators such as cats and foxes from getting in. If it is not possible to permanently attach their shelter to their living enclosure, guinea pigs should be given the opportunity to run and explore every day.

Some people prefer to keep their guinea pigs indoors, in a large enclosure that has room for them to exercise and several places in which they can sleep, rest and hide. The decision on whether indoor living is suitable for your pets depends on their temperaments, previous lifestyle and experience, and whether they are able to adjust to living inside.

You should also make sure that there is plenty for your guinea pigs to do. They are intelligent animals, so if they are bored they may suffer. For more about toys and activities to keep your pets occupied, see page 30.

A good location

Your guinea pigs' home should be located in a quiet, calm place. Guinea pigs can easily be frightened and can become stressed if they are housed where there is a lot of noise and activity.

If your guinea pigs are living in an outdoor home, make sure that it is raised off the ground to stop it getting damp. You will also need to ensure that it is well ventilated, weatherproof and escape-proof. Their home and additional enclosures should be placed away from any draughts, heat and direct sunlight. Wherever possible, when temperatures drop below 15°C guinea pigs should be housed indoors. If they have to be kept outside, they must be provided with sufficient bedding throughout the whole enclosure to enable them to keep warm, and a cover for the shelter is advised.

An indoor home should be placed in a quiet spot away from televisions and other noise. It should also be away from direct heat such as radiators and sunny windows, and protected from draughts. A room temperature of 17–20°C is ideal. If your home is centrally heated some areas may get too hot, which can cause heat stroke in guinea pigs.

Hiding places

Because guinea pigs are prey animals, as well as their main shelter they should also have constant access to hiding places, where they can go to be alone or if they feel afraid. These can include tunnels, shelters and cardboard boxes. You will need to make sure there is at least one per pet so that there are enough places for them all to hide at the same time. It is also best to provide a hiding place that is big enough for all your guinea pigs to snuggle up in together if they want to. You can find out more about hiding places on page 28.

Suitable bedding

Guinea pigs need plenty of bedding to keep them warm and comfortable. Line the bottom of their shelter (or enclosure, if you have indoor guinea pigs) with newspaper and a layer of dust-free

wood shavings. Soft woods such as pine should not be used as these can make your guinea pigs ill. Provide plenty of dust-free hay on top. Check your guinea pigs' main shelter regularly to ensure it is still weatherproof, as leaks or damp will quickly affect the health of your guinea pigs. In winter you will need to check that they have plenty of extra bedding to keep them warm and dry, and if temperatures fall below 15°C, ideally you should move your guinea pigs indoors.

Toileting and cleaning

Guinea pigs need constant access to a suitable toileting area. This should be separate from where they sleep. Toileting areas should be cleaned every day to make sure they have clean, dry bedding. The whole of the rest of your guinea pigs' home should be thoroughly cleaned weekly, or more frequently if it is excessively soiled, using non-toxic, pet-safe cleaning products. Make sure their home is thoroughly dried and, to reduce stress, add a small amount of the used, unsoiled bedding back into the enclosure so that it smells familiar to your pets.

Toys, exercise and activities

Guinea pigs are intelligent, inquisitive animals and need plenty of toys and activities to enrich their lives. If your guinea pigs do not have permanent access to somewhere they can run, ▶

TOP: Line your guinea pigs' shelter with a thick layer of bedding. BELOW: Familiar-smelling bedding can help to reassure your guinea pigs while travelling. RIGHT: Toys will give your guinea pigs something to explore and investigate.

explore and play, then they need to have the chance to do this away from their shelter on a daily basis. You can do this by providing your guinea pigs with access to a large exercise run. Ensure it is secure and predator-proof with appropriate hiding places, and provide water and food.

There are lots of different toys available that can be put into the enclosure or run to provide your guinea pigs with opportunities for physical exercise and mental stimulation. Items such as tunnels, cardboard boxes with holes in them and large cardboard tubes stuffed with hay are perfect for keeping your guinea pigs amused. Choose toys for your guinea pigs with care and check them regularly for signs of damage or wear and tear to avoid any chance of injury. For more on toys, see page 30.

Transporting your guinea pigs

It is very important to think about how you will transport your guinea pigs safely when you are bringing them home or taking them to the vet. Travelling can be stressful for guinea pigs and so should be kept to a minimum unless absolutely necessary. There are several ways in which you can make their journey more comfortable and ensure that they are safe in your vehicle.

Being enclosed will make them feel safer, so choose a well-ventilated, robust plastic carrier with solid sides rather than a wire cage for your guinea pigs to travel in. A cardboard carrier is not a good idea, because your guinea pigs could chew through it and escape, or it could disintegrate if it gets wet. Guinea pigs that live together should be transported in the same carrier, so make sure that the one you choose is large enough for them all. Travelling together eases the journey and also means that any unfamiliar scents in the carrier will be transferred to all your guinea pigs, which can avoid any problems and the need for pets to be reintroduced after a time

apart. A hiding place that is large enough for all your guinea pigs and familiar-smelling items, such as bedding, in the carrier can help reassure your guinea pigs while they are on the move.

Give your guinea pigs plenty of fresh water and hay for the journey and check on them regularly. Place the carrier on the seat sideways on, secured with the seatbelt, or place it in the footwell behind the seat. It can get unbearably hot in a car on a sunny day, even when it is not that warm, so be aware of this when you are transporting your guinea pigs. Do not leave them alone in a vehicle, as the temperature can quickly soar to levels that can be fatal.

When your guinea pigs are back home, put your pets in their home and allow them to rest for a while without being disturbed. This is particularly important when they come home for the first time, so they can get used to their new surroundings. You can download an advice sheet on transporting guinea pigs from www.rspca.org.uk/guinea pigs/environment.

Holidays

When you go away on holiday, it is better that you find a responsible adult to care for and meet all your guinea pigs' welfare needs in their own home. If you are unable to do so, there are many boarding facilities that you can use. If this is your option, visit it beforehand to make sure you are confident that they are able to give your guinea pigs the appropriate care they need and will meet all of their five welfare needs (see page 5). You can ease your guinea pigs' move there by keeping them together and ensuring that they have familiar-smelling items such as toys and some of their bedding with them. Make sure the boarding facility has access to a vet who has expertise in guinea pigs.

Diet

2

Make sure your guinea pigs have a well-balanced diet.

What to feed your guinea pigs

A healthy diet

To stay fit and healthy, your guinea pigs need constant access to fresh, clean water and a well-balanced diet of grass hay, leafy green vegetables and nuggets. How much an individual guinea pig needs to eat depends on their age, lifestyle and general health. If you have any concerns or queries about feeding, your vet will be able to give you detailed advice on what, and how much, to feed your guinea pigs.

Water bottle and food bowl

Before you bring your guinea pigs home, you will need to buy a good-quality drip-feed bottle. Always give your guinea pigs clean, fresh water and make sure it is changed at least once a day. When you are changing the water, wash the bottle and nozzle thoroughly to avoid contamination and check it for leaks and blockages. In winter you must also make sure that your guinea pigs' water doesn't freeze.

Guinea pigs generally stay on all fours to feed, so their food container must be on the ground or just above it. The best choice is a metal J-feeder, which can be attached to the wire door of their home. A heavy ceramic bowl can also be used, as it cannot be knocked over. Plastic bowls should be avoided, as they can be tipped or chewed. It is very important to make sure that the food bowl is suitably sized for your guinea pigs. If it is too big it is easy to overfill it. Overfeeding your guinea pigs in this way can lead to weight gain and health issues. Get into the routine of washing your guinea pigs' bowl every day, to avoid contamination ▶

from urine or faeces. When you put it back in their home, you should also check that they have plenty of fresh hay and remove any uneaten or soiled food from the enclosure to stop it spoiling.

The first few days

A rehoming centre or breeder should provide detailed information that will tell you what type of food your guinea pigs have been eating so far and will outline their feeding routine. They should also supply a few days' food for your guinea pigs. Whenever possible, follow the feeding notes while your guinea pigs are settling in, and stick to the type of food and routine they are used to. Once settled, any changes in your guinea pigs' diet should only be made gradually, as a sudden swap in brand or type of food could upset their digestive system and make them very ill. If you have any concerns or queries about feeding, your vet will be able to give you detailed advice on what, and how much, to feed your guinea pigs.

ABOVE: Clean, fresh water is essential for your guinea pigs. RIGHT: Guinea pigs need constant access to hay and grass.

Grazing

Guinea pigs are grazers and naturally eat only grass, herbs and some plants like dandelions and groundsels. Guinea pigs will eat for long periods of time throughout the day and night, as they only sleep for short periods. A guinea pig's digestive system needs hay and grass in order to work properly, so this should make up the majority of

their diet and be available continuously. Grazing on hay and grass is also vital to keep a guinea pig's teeth healthy and at the correct length and shape.

Hay and leafy greens

Good-quality hay must be freely available at all times. Choose sweet-smelling grass hay, such as Timothy hay, that is dust-free, and allow at least a guinea pig-sized amount for each of your pets every day. Guinea pigs also need a variety of safe, washed leafy greens such as kale, cabbage, spinach and broccoli every day. These are excellent sources of vitamin C for your guinea pigs. Never give your guinea pigs lawnmower clippings, citrus fruits (such as oranges or grapefruit), starchy foods (such as potato) or vegetables that grow from bulbs (such as onions, garlic or leeks). All of these can upset their digestive system and make them ill.

Muesli-style foods

Muesli-style foods are associated with health problems in guinea pigs because they tend to feed selectively on one or two elements of the food and then eat less hay alongside it. Together, these two factors make for an unbalanced diet. Muesli-style food can also lead to teeth and stomach problems as well as make your guinea pigs overweight.

If you are supplementing your guinea pigs' diet of leafy greens and hay with muesli, it would be best to replace the muesli with nuggets. This transition should be done gradually over several weeks, with detailed advice from your vet, to avoid making your guinea pigs ill.

Nuggets

Nuggets are an important part of your guinea pigs' diet; they provide vitamin C and other nutrients they need to stay healthy. A fresh portion of guinea pig nuggets should be available daily, as per the manufacturer's instructions. Vitamin C is destroyed over time and more quickly with exposure to the air, so the nuggets must be changed every day – do not just top up the bowl. Buy small sealed bags of food and, once opened, store them in an airtight container. Always use them by the best-before date.

Remember that growing, pregnant, nursing or underweight guinea pigs may need a larger portion of nuggets. Your vet will be able to advise you about how to provide the best diet for each of your guinea pigs.

Treats

A guinea pig's diet doesn't naturally include cereals, root vegetables or fruit. However, offering occasional healthy treats in moderation, such as small amounts of carrot, apple, melon and cucumber, can add variety and interest to their diet. It can also be a good way to develop your relationship with your guinea pigs. Do not feed them sugary treats, though, as these may harm them. Make ▶

FAR LEFT: Leafy greens such as spinach, cabbage and kale are excellent sources of vitamin C.
LEFT: RSPCA Healthy Nuggets for Guinea Pigs.

ABOVE: Treats in moderation can help you to build a relationship with your guinea pigs. RIGHT: In the wild, guinea pigs graze and forage for food. BELOW: New foods should be introduced slowly and in small amounts.

sure that any soiled or uneaten food is removed from the enclosure to stop it spoiling.

New foods

Not all green leafy plants are safe to feed to your guinea pigs, and some can be extremely poisonous. Your vet can advise you on what is safe, but if you are in any doubt, leave it out! If your guinea pigs are trying a new (safe) leafy plant, it is best to give them a small amount to start with, to make sure they can tolerate it. If you see any signs of an upset stomach, such as loose droppings, it is best to avoid that particular food.

Making meals fun

There are many ways in which you can make your guinea pigs' mealtimes fun. In the wild, guinea pigs forage for food and graze, so you can encourage these behaviours by scattering their greens and daily ration of nuggets around their home.

Try hiding food in cardboard

boxes or tubes for them to discover easily. Alternatively, you could fill puzzle feeders and balls with hay, grass or nuggets to add variety to their mealtime hunts. Do make sure, however, that there are enough feeders for each of your guinea pigs.

Chewing can be encouraged by using wooden chew sticks designed for guinea pigs, or by using branches from untreated fruit trees.

Eating droppings (caecotrophy)

Guinea pigs produce two types of droppings. You may see a guinea pig eating softer droppings directly from their bottom. Eating these is an essential part of their diet, because it helps them to get as much goodness as possible from their food. Your guinea pigs will also produce waste in the form of hard droppings.

Weight watch

Remember that the majority of your guinea pigs' diet should be made up of grass hay and leafy greens such as kale, cabbage and spinach. You can help your guinea pigs to maintain a healthy weight by limiting treats, such as apple and carrot, and by ensuring that they are not over-fed on nuggets. If a guinea pig eats more food than they need, or too much of the wrong food, they will become overweight, develop teeth and stomach problems and may suffer.

How much an individual guinea pig needs to eat depends on their age, lifestyle and state of health, so if necessary adjust how much you feed each guinea pig to make sure they do not become underweight or overweight. Do remember that young guinea pigs, and pregnant and nursing females, will have different needs to other guinea pigs. It is a good idea to note your guinea pigs' weight and keep a careful eye on them by weighing them regularly. Any changes could be indicative of health problems, especially dental disease. Your vet will be able to give you detailed advice about how to give your guinea pigs a balanced diet, with any adjustments that may need to be made for their individual circumstances. You can find out more about keeping your guinea pigs at a healthy weight at www.rspca.org.uk/guineapigs/diet.

Changes in habits

Take note of the amounts that your guinea pigs eat and drink every day, and watch for any changes in an individual's eating, drinking or toileting habits. For example, if they are having difficulty in eating, have stopped eating or there is a reduction in the amount of droppings, or they stop, or if there are soft droppings sticking to their back end or lying around the cage, talk to your vet straight away as they could be ill.

Things to avoid

Be aware that there are also many wild plants such as dock, bluebells and ragwort, as well as garden plants such as ivy, foxglove, oleander, crocuses, daffodils and tulips, that are poisonous to guinea pigs. There is more on poisonous substances on page 43. If you are not sure whether a plant is safe for your guinea pigs, do not give it to them. If you think your guinea pigs may have eaten something poisonous, speak to your vet immediately.

ABOVE: Your vet can show you how to perform health and weight checks.

Behaviour

3

Getting to know each of your guinea pigs' normal habits and behaviour will help you spot any problems.

Guinea pig behaviour

Guinea pigs are very sociable and inquisitive animals and need to interact with other friendly guinea pigs as well as people. They are also active for up to 20 hours during the day and night, only sleeping for short periods. This means it is very important that your pets are able to access the things that they need at all times, such as space, food and water, companion guinea pigs and toys, which ensure that they can stay healthy and behave normally. Understanding your guinea pigs' behaviour and knowing what is normal for each of them is vital. It will help you to identify any changes that may indicate that they are ill or in pain.

Staying fit, happy and healthy

Guinea pigs need regular and frequent opportunities to exercise every day. Ideally, they should have permanent access to their living enclosure so that they can move freely between this and their main shelter. This will help your pets to behave normally by giving them the space they need to leap, run and chase each other as well as tunnel through hay, forage and gnaw things. You may also see them suddenly jumping with all four feet off the ground, often turning 90 degrees in mid-air. This is called 'pop-corning'. It is usually seen when your pigs are excited, but they may also do this if they are very frightened and running away from something. ▶

◀ Guinea pigs are intelligent, inquisitive animals, so make sure your pets have an interesting environment in which there is plenty to do. This will give your guinea pigs plenty of mental and physical stimulation so that they are more likely to remain fit, healthy and happy. As guinea pigs do not usually climb or jump over vertical objects, it is best if their enclosure is on one level, with plenty of space for toys and hiding places as well as room to exercise.

Hiding places

It is natural for guinea pigs to be cautious when they are placed in a new environment or when they encounter a stranger. If they hear a loud noise or see something that frightens them, guinea pigs stop what they are doing and become very alert. They may make short vibrating sounds to warn their companions and stay completely still for a while, or, if they decide the threat is too near or frightening, they will run away to a safe hiding place.

It is essential, therefore, to provide enough hiding places for each of your guinea pigs, plus one that is large enough for them to hide in together if they want to. Hiding places should be positioned in a quiet area, away from draughts and direct sunlight. They should be large enough for a guinea pig to move swiftly underneath, but still low enough to give them a sense of security. Hiding places should have two exits, to prevent a dominant guinea pig becoming territorial or aggressive towards the others inside. For your guinea pigs to feel that their hiding places remain safe and secure it is extremely important that you do not remove them from it, or trap them inside it.

Being sociable

In the wild, guinea pigs live in social groups of up to 10 individuals. Because of this, it is essential that your pets are able to interact with other friendly guinea pigs, unless advised otherwise by a vet or suitable behavioural expert. Watching your guinea pigs' body language and postures towards each other as they interact can help you to understand how they are feeling. A friendly encounter between guinea pigs starts with an approach, when they will sniff each other, then they will edge closer so they are whisker to whisker. This is known as 'nosing'.

Your pets may also like to rest closely together, which can help them keep warm, and groom one another, which helps to strengthen their bond. Some meetings are less friendly – especially those between competitive males. There is more on this on page 35.

Chatting
Guinea pigs are very chatty pets and they communicate using around 11 different noises, such as the well-known 'wheek-wheek' noise, which is a sign of excitement or a call to find a friend, through to a low 'purring' sound when they are relaxed or seeking contact. Often, when your guinea pigs are exploring, you may hear them make a series of short 'putt-putt' or 'chutt' noises. If your guinea pig chatters their teeth, this can be a warning signal that they are feeling angry, unhappy or frustrated and need some space. If you hear your guinea pigs squealing, this shows they are scared or in pain. As you get to know your pets better, you will start to recognize all of these different noises. Knowing what they mean can help you to understand what each of your guinea pigs is feeling.

Scent marking
Guinea pigs use scent secretions, which are made by dragging their bottom across the ground, or urinating on each other, as ways to communicate. They also scent-mark by rubbing their chin or cheeks across things, such as their shelter or tunnel. Both help make their homes smell familiar and reassuring. These scents are not detected by people, though. This is why it is important when you are cleaning your guinea pigs' home that you transfer some of the old, unsoiled bedding back into the enclosure, so that it still smells familiar and safe to them. Where possible, if a guinea pig needs to be removed from the enclosure to travel, such as to the vet for a health check-up, it is best to transport them with their companions. This ensures that scents remain familiar and helps avoid potential problems associated with reintroducing guinea pigs after time apart.

When there are problems

Every guinea pig is different and the way they behave will depend upon their age, as well as their personality and experiences. However, it is important to make sure that you are very familiar with the normal behaviour and routine of each of your guinea pigs, as this will help you to quickly identify any changes that could indicate that they are frightened, bored, ill or in pain. Keep a close eye on your guinea pigs and watch for some of the following signs that can suggest your pet is stressed: changes in their eating or toileting habits, hiding, being aggressive, chewing their cage bars, changes in grooming, playing with their water bottle, repeatedly circling the enclosure, sitting hunched up or being reluctant to move.

If you see these behaviours in any of your guinea pigs, consult your vet so they can give your pet a check-up and rule out any illnesses. Your vet may refer you to a suitable behavioural expert for advice. You can find links to information about finding a behavioural expert on page 47, or by going to www.rspca.org.uk/findabehaviourist. Always be quiet and gentle when you are around your guinea pigs. Never shout at or punish them as they are very unlikely to understand and can become more nervous or scared. If your guinea pigs' behaviour becomes an ongoing problem, talk to an expert.

Toys

Toys enrich your guinea pigs' environment by making it more interesting. It also helps your pets perform normal behaviours, such as chewing and investigating. As well as shop-bought toys, there are many inexpensive ways to add items to your guinea pigs' enclosure.

When you add new toys and objects to your guinea pigs' home, do it with care. Keep a close eye on your pets to check that they are not stressed or frightened. If they seem very unsure or scared, remove the object or toy. As you get to know your guinea pigs, you will find that they will each have a preference for different toys, so experiment until you find the ones they like best. Make sure there are enough items for each guinea pig,

Toys add interest to your guinea pigs' environment.

allowance into a cardboard tube or a box can also encourage your guinea pigs to explore.

TUNNELS You can purchase tunnels for guinea pigs that are made of fabric. You can also make them yourself from cardboard boxes, cardboard tubes and large pipes. Make sure they are big enough for each of your guinea pigs.

OBJECTS TO MANIPULATE
Untreated straw/wicker/seagrass mats and baskets and balls are ideal for guinea pigs to investigate. If you can, try hiding some of your guinea pigs' food in or under these toys to encourage foraging behaviour.

to avoid competition and one of them monopolizing a favourite item.

Do not go toy mad, though; there needs to be a balance between providing interesting items and overfilling their enclosure, because your guinea pigs need plenty of space to exercise in easily.

Here are some ideas to try:

PAPER Give your guinea pigs shredded non-glossy newspaper or paper bags with the handles removed, or bundle up your guinea pigs' favourite food item in brown paper as a parcel for them to discover.

CARDBOARD Cut holes into boxes to make hiding places. Tucking hay or healthy treats from their daily food

SAFETY FIRST Make sure anything you give your guinea pigs is safe and suitable for their use. Materials should be non-toxic with smooth, rounded edges. Inspect toys regularly and discard any that are damaged or dangerous. Do not provide your guinea pigs with blankets, as these animals have a tendency to chew them, which could result in an intestinal blockage.

Company

4

Being with others

Guinea pigs are naturally sociable and normally prefer to live in pairs or in a group. Unless you have been specifically advised otherwise by a vet or suitable behavioural expert, always house your guinea pigs in pairs or in a group, as a guinea pig left on its own can suffer and may develop abnormal behaviours.

Handle your guinea pigs gently every day.

A good mix

One of the reasons why people had concerns about keeping guinea pigs in pairs or groups in the past was the risk of unwanted pregnancy. However, nowadays this can be prevented with a simple operation to neuter male guinea pigs.

A good combination of guinea pigs is a neutered male with one or more females. Make sure the male is neutered before they are housed together, unless you are intending to breed from the group and sufficient provisions have been made to care for both parents and offspring.

It is not common to neuter females as the operation is more complicated, but if you are going to keep single-sex pairs, two females can live together quite happily. Two males may also successfully live as a pair if they are brothers and have been brought up together. It is still advisable to get them neutered to reduce fighting, though. For more on neutering, go to www.rspca.org.uk/neutering.

Introducing new guinea pigs

The best pairing or group of guinea pigs are animals that were born in the same litter and have been raised together. However, if you want to bring in another guinea pig to live with one you have already, it may be possible to introduce them to each other, although male guinea pigs should be neutered first.

Pairing guinea pigs takes time and patience, and it is not always successful. It can be stressful and must be done gradually and under supervision, preferably in a space that is new to both animals. It is therefore recommended that pairing is done by experts who will be able to spot any signs that a guinea pig is stressed and unhappy. You can seek expert advice on pairing from a rescue organization such as the RSPCA, or another rehoming centre specializing in guinea pigs. They can find suitable guinea pigs for you and may also have established pairs or groups ready for rehoming.

Pecking order

Guinea pigs kept together will naturally form a 'pecking order', with some animals being more dominant than others. Establishing positions in a pair or group helps to prevent aggression in the future. Male guinea pigs will challenge each other for dominant status by teeth chattering and standing in a threatening position with their heads moving forward. Usually this is enough and it does not lead to more aggressive behaviour; however, it is a good reason why you should keep a single male with one or more females, as it usually makes for a happier pairing or group. It is also important to make sure that all your guinea pigs have access to hiding places where they can go to get away from each other if they want to, otherwise they can become stressed.

Guinea pigs and rabbits

Guinea pigs and rabbits have different welfare needs, so keeping them together is not advised. Rabbits also harbour bacteria that can result in breathing problems in guinea pigs. The best companion for a guinea pig is another friendly guinea pig. For further information, including advice on what to do if you already have a guinea pig and a rabbit living together, visit www.rspca.org.uk/rabbitsandguineapigs.

Other pets

Cats and dogs can view your guinea pigs as prey and chase them. Never leave your guinea pigs unsupervised with another animal or person who may (deliberately or accidentally) harm or frighten them.

You and your guinea pigs

A good relationship with your guinea pigs can be rewarding for both you and your pets. It also helps when you have to catch and transport your animals for health checks and routine examinations by your vet. Guinea pigs that are slowly and gradually introduced to people in a positive way can learn to be relaxed around them. Taking the time to handle your guinea pigs gently every day from an early age will help them to learn to value and enjoy your company.

If for any reason your vet or a suitable behavioural expert has advised you that one of your pets has to be kept on their own, it is especially important that you interact positively with your guinea pig every day and provide plenty to do, so that they stay happy and healthy. ▶

ABOVE: Teach your children to be gentle with your guinea pigs.
RIGHT: Learn to handle your guinea pigs correctly.

Your guinea pigs' reaction to being handled is likely to depend on their past experiences. This is especially true of guinea pigs who are not used to being handled or have been handled roughly, as they may find human contact distressing. This can be expressed as fearfulness, escape behaviour or aggression. With time and patience you can help your guinea pigs grow more confident and comfortable around people. If you are concerned about anything to do with handling your guinea pigs, go to page 47 or ask your vet or a suitable behavioural expert for advice.

Handling your guinea pigs

When you first bring your guinea pigs home, they may be nervous, so do not attempt to handle them. For the first few days, simply talk quietly to them. Encourage them to approach you by offering healthy treats, then you can start to gently stroke them. When they become more comfortable and confident with this, you can gradually get them used to being picked up.

To pick them up safely, using both hands, place one hand under your guinea pig's chest so their front legs are either side of your fingers, and use your other hand to support the back and rear. This should all be done very gently, as grabbing and gripping too firmly around the stomach and chest could injure them.

Be patient when beginning to handle your guinea pigs to allow your pet to grow confident and comfortable around you. To avoid startling your guinea pigs, always move slowly and talk quietly around them.

Once they get to know you, your guinea pigs will enjoy spending time with you, but not all guinea pigs will like being picked up and held. For those that are afraid, or are not happy and relaxed when they are handled, it is best if all interactions are carried out at ground level, as people are likely to be perceived as less threatening to your guinea pigs when in this position.

Training your guinea pigs

Guinea pigs are intelligent animals, so training them is another great way to spend time together and enhance your bond. They can be taught a variety of things, such as coming when called, entering their shelter on cue and retrieving objects, all of which provide important mental and physical stimulation for your pets. Only positive, reward-based methods such as clicker training should be used. Consulting a suitable behavioural expert or someone who is knowledgeable about reward-based training may be useful when you are learning how to train your guinea pigs effectively.

Guinea pigs and children

Many families with children keep guinea pigs. Having a pet can improve a child's social skills, and caring for an animal can encourage kindness, understanding and responsibility. While children will quickly learn to treat new guinea pigs as part of the family, it is important to teach them to handle them gently and carefully. Always supervise your children when they are handling guinea pigs, and minimize the risk of them accidentally dropping your pets by getting them to sit on the ground to pet or hold them. Only adults and responsible older children should be allowed to pick up guinea pigs.

Safety first

Never leave your guinea pigs unsupervised with a person who may deliberately or accidentally harm or frighten them. When you are away, make sure your pets are properly cared for by a responsible person who can give them the care and company they need.

If one of your guinea pigs shows any changes in behaviour, or shows regular signs of stress or fear, such as hiding or aggression, when they are being handled, get them checked by a vet to rule out any form of illness or injury that could be causing their reaction. If necessary, your vet may refer your pet to a suitable behavioural expert.

Health
and welfare

5

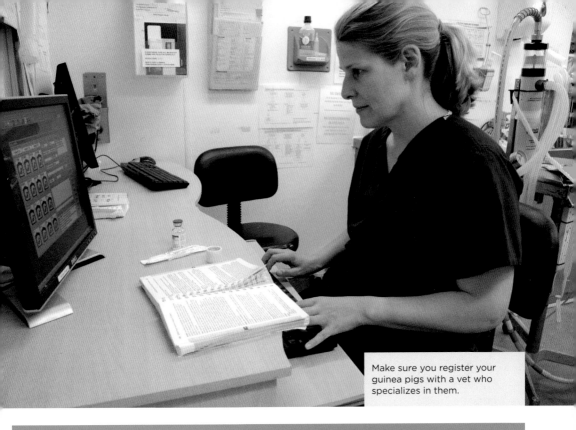

Make sure you register your guinea pigs with a vet who specializes in them.

Protecting your pet

Signs of illness or pain in guinea pigs can be difficult to spot. It is vital that you get to know your guinea pigs really well by familiarizing yourself with their normal, healthy behaviour. Check your guinea pigs daily for changes in behaviour and signs of injury or illness, and make sure someone else does this if you are away. If you see any changes that may indicate that they are ill or injured, you should contact your vet immediately.

Find a vet and arrange insurance
Guinea pigs are very different to cats, dogs and other animals, so it is important that you find a vet who specializes in guinea pigs with whom you can register your new pets, and book them in for a check-up. They will be able to give you lots of information on looking after your guinea pigs, and neutering them if they are male, as well as detailed general pet-care advice. You can read more about finding a vet and low-cost vet care at www.rspca.org.uk/whatwedo/vetcare.

Check the insurance situation, too. Some charities and breeders may provide a short period of insurance cover, which you can either take over and extend, or you may want to arrange an alternative ▶

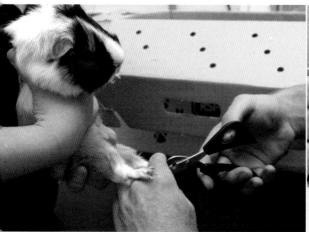

ABOVE: Groom your guinea pigs regularly. LEFT: Check your guinea pigs' nails at least once a week.

policy. Where insurance is not provided, it is a good idea to think about arranging for an insurance policy to start from the moment you bring your guinea pigs home.

Health checks

Take your guinea pigs for a routine health check with your vet at least once a year. It is a good opportunity to ask for advice about things you can do to protect your guinea pigs' health, including dental checks. Unlike dogs, cats and rabbits, guinea pigs are not usually given routine vaccinations.

It is important to carry out daily health checks at home, too. You can do this as part of the normal handling of your pets; for example, when grooming them or playing with them. It is important to check them all over to make sure they are healthy, and also take some time to make sure they are behaving normally and eating well. Don't forget to weigh them regularly, too, and write down their weight somewhere safe so that you can check for any changes.

Grooming

Regular grooming allows you to check your guinea pigs' coat and overall body condition. It is important for all guinea pigs that grooming is introduced positively and gradually. If you are not sure how to groom your guinea pigs properly, talk to a pet-care specialist. This is especially important in the case of long-haired breeds, which will need grooming daily. If your guinea pigs suddenly become reluctant to be groomed, you should talk to your vet, as your pets may be ill.

Teeth

A guinea pig's teeth grow continuously for the whole of their life, and therefore need to be worn down and kept at the correct length and shape by eating grass, hay and leafy green plants. A poor diet, changes to the environment, injury and other causes of stress can alter eating habits, which can lead to an overgrowth of teeth. A guinea pig's teeth should be checked regularly, because dental problems can become very serious without prompt treatment. If your guinea pigs' teeth are overgrown or misaligned, or if you notice a change in their eating habits, difficulty eating, excessive drooling or a wet chin, you must see a vet who specializes in guinea pigs immediately.

Nails

A guinea pig's nails should be checked at least once a week because they grow quickly and may get too long. If they are overgrown or damaged, your vet will be able to deal with them.

Vitamin C deficiency

Guinea pigs cannot make their own vitamin C, nor can they store it for long periods. This means that they must be able to get their daily requirement of vitamin C from the food they eat. Signs that your guinea pigs may be suffering from a lack of vitamin C include lameness, lethargy, pain upon handling, excessive salivation and not eating. The indications are generally more severe in young animals. Vitamin C deficiency is easily prevented by giving your guinea pigs a good diet that includes foods such as kale, cabbage, broccoli and nuggets, which are all good sources of vitamin C.

Flystrike

Flystrike occurs when flies lay their eggs in the fur of animals, particularly around their bottom. The maggots hatch and eat their way into the guinea pig's skin. Flystrike can occur in hours; toxic shock and death can result very quickly. Make sure that you clean your guinea pigs' toilet areas every day, and clean their housing and change their bedding at least once a week. In warm weather check the fur and skin around your guinea pigs' rear ends twice a day, as urine staining or droppings that are stuck will attract flies. If your pet's back end is dirty, clean it immediately with warm water and ensure the area is dried thoroughly. Speak to your vet about the best way of reducing the risk of flystrike before warmer weather starts. For more information, go to www.rspca.org.uk/flystrike.

Constipation and diarrhoea

Both of these conditions can have a number of different causes and can be very serious and rapidly fatal to a guinea pig. If the quantity of droppings your pets produce reduces, stops or they become loose, you must seek immediate veterinary help.

Urinary tract infections

Cystitis, a urinary tract infection, is fairly common in guinea pigs but is difficult to spot until it is quite severe. Signs include a hunched posture and squealing whilst urinating, as well as blood in the urine. Immediate veterinary treatment is ▶

◀ required, but infections can be prevented by providing a good diet.

Breathing problems

Bacteria can cause breathing problems in guinea pigs. Without prompt treatment, breathing problems may develop into pneumonia, which can be fatal. Guinea pigs can catch the bacteria from other animals and are more prone to illness if kept in damp, overcrowded conditions. If you notice one of your guinea pigs has laboured breathing, a loss of appetite and a discharge from the nose, it is important to see your vet immediately to stop it developing into something more serious.

Ringworm

Ringworm is a highly contagious fungal infection of the skin that guinea pigs can catch from an infected animal or infected bedding. If you notice bald patches with red crusty areas on one of your guinea pigs' face or back, speak to your vet immediately. It is important to get ringworm treated promptly so that it does not become infected. Ringworm is very contagious and it is possible for people to catch it from an infected guinea pig, so it is extremely important that you wash your hands thoroughly in hot soapy water after handling your pets.

Mites, ticks and lice

Parasites such as mites, ticks and lice can cause scratching and distress to your guinea pigs, so if they appear, it is vital that you seek prompt veterinary treatment. Regular grooming will help you to spot signs of parasites so you can treat them quickly. A guinea pig that scratches or rubs its ears, or shakes its head, may have an infestation of ear mites. Other mites, such as fur mites, forage mites and harvest mites (also known as mange), can live on the skin, causing extreme irritation and distress to animals. When you are grooming your guinea pigs, check for lice eggs or ticks in their fur. Do not attempt to remove a tick yourself. Your vet will be able to advise you of suitable treatments for both mites and lice and will be able to safely remove a tick. If you notice any of these signs, contact your vet immediately for prompt treatment.

Pododermatitis (bumblefoot)

Swollen and sore foot pads, known as bumblefoot, are quite common in guinea pigs and are usually caused by bacteria getting into the skin through small cuts or scrapes. To prevent bumblefoot, it is important to house your guinea pigs in an enclosure with a solid floor, not a wire base; one which is not abrasive. Keep your pets at a healthy weight, as

overweight guinea pigs are more prone to this condition, and make sure that toilet areas are cleaned daily and the rest of their home is cleaned at least weekly with products that are safe for your pets. Check your guinea pigs' feet regularly for signs of sores or red patches, as it is important to get these treated promptly by your vet to avoid any serious complications.

Stress

Guinea pigs that are stressed are much more likely to become ill, so try to minimize unnecessary stress and provide constant access to safe hiding places and a predictable routine. Keep a close eye on your guinea pigs' behaviour, eating and drinking habits and droppings. If these change or your pets are showing signs of fear or stress, seek advice from your vet or a suitable behavioural expert.

Poisoning

Preventing your guinea pigs from coming into contact with poisonous substances and treating any accidental poisonings quickly and appropriately is an important part of responsible pet ownership. Common items that are poisonous to guinea pigs include rodent poisons – also known as 'rodenticides' – ivy, foxgloves, ragwort, dock, bluebells, crocuses, daffodils, chocolate and glyphosphate herbicide products. Never give your guinea pigs greens picked from the side of the road, as they may have been sprayed with pesticides which could be fatal to your pets.

If you suspect your pet has been poisoned, act fast and contact your nearest vet for advice immediately. For more detailed advice on preventing and dealing with poisoning, go to www.rspca.org.uk/poisoning.

CLOCKWISE FROM TOP LEFT: Items poisonous to guinea pigs: chocolate, slug pellets, foxgloves, bluebells, daffodils and herbicides.

Your questions answered

Dr Samantha Gaines BSc (Hons) MSc PhD, guinea pig behaviour and welfare expert, Companion Animals Department, RSPCA

Q: What should I be looking for when checking over my guinea pigs?

A: When you give your guinea pigs a daily check, you are looking to see that they are healthy and behaving normally. Watching your guinea pigs feeding will help you see that they are eating their normal amount without any difficulty. Make sure that their chin is not wet and they are not drooling, which could suggest dental problems. Check their eyes, ears and nose to make sure there is no discharge, and their feet to check there are no sores or cuts. Their breathing should be regular and quiet, and they should move well without any lameness or appearing to be in pain. You should also check that their teeth and nails are the correct length, without any damage, and that they are toileting happily without any changes. Grooming gives you a good opportunity to check that their coat and skin are in good condition and that they are the right weight. You should weigh them and record the amount regularly so that you can spot any changes immediately. The more time you spend with your guinea pigs, the more familiar you will become with their behaviour and the easier it will be to spot if something is wrong.

Q: I had two female guinea pigs but one recently died. I would like to get another; how should I do this?

A: Guinea pigs are sociable animals and enjoy one another's company, so your guinea pig is likely to be missing having another one around. As your guinea pig is a girl it should be possible to introduce another guinea pig to her without too many problems. For example, another female might prove a good companion, or a young neutered male. To ensure that you find the right combination and that the introduction is successful, it is best to do this with the help of a guinea pig expert. There are organizations you can contact that specialize in rehoming guinea pigs – they can help you find a suitable companion and make sure that the introduction goes well.

Q: One of my guinea pigs is chewing the hair of the other. Why?
A: When a guinea pig chews their own hair or that of another animal in their group, it can cause bald patches and you may also see bite marks in the skin. This is called 'barbering' and is usually as a result of stress, or a guinea pig bullying others. It is important to get your vet to check over your guinea pigs to rule out any other causes, such as skin infections. You can also provide more enrichment in the enclosure to ensure that your guinea pigs have enough to do, as well as providing enough hiding

places for each of your pets, so that they can avoid anything they find scary. If the behaviour continues despite all of this, you should consult a suitable behaviour expert with knowledge of guinea pigs who should be able to help you identify the cause of the behaviour and advise you on how to improve it.

Q: I have just recently adopted a pair of guinea pigs from the RSPCA, but they are very nervous. What can I do to help them feel more confident?
A: As guinea pigs are prey animals it is normal for them to find people a bit scary, but with time and patience they can become less fearful. Many learn very quickly that their owner brings tasty food; so much so that they will run to them squeaking once they see them! It is important to go slowly and to build up their confidence over a period of time. A good way to do this is to give them something

tasty every time you go to see them so that their association with you is positive. Make sure you move slowly and talk quietly when around them to avoid scaring them. Over time they should become increasingly relaxed in your presence and begin to value and enjoy your company.

BELOW: Giving your guinea pigs treats can help them to feel relaxed in your presence. LEFT: Check that your guinea pigs are happy and healthy every day.

Index

Resources

RSPCA

For more information and advice from the RSPCA about caring for your guinea pigs, go to www.rspca.org.uk/guineapigs.

Veterinary advice

- Vet Help Direct is an online guide to help you decide how quickly you should contact your vet. Go to www.vethelpdirect.com.

- Vetfone is a 24-hour service, like an NHS Direct for pets. It is staffed exclusively by UK-qualified veterinary nurses. Go to www.vetfone.co.uk.

- Find a Vet. All veterinary surgeons must be registered by the Royal College of Veterinary Surgeons (RCVS). Go to www.findavet.rcvs.org.uk/home.

Behaviour Advice

- The Association for the Study of Animal Behaviour (ASAB) accredits Certified Clinical Animal Behaviourists (CCAB) who possess an Honours or higher degree in a relevant subject, have attended specialist courses, and have at least three years' regular clinical experience. Go to www.asab.org.

- The Association of Pet Behaviour Counsellors (APBC) also represents animal behaviourists. APBC members have a relevant degree and at least two years' experience. Go to www.apbc.org.uk

- If you are concerned about your guinea pigs' behaviour, contact a major rescue organization or rehoming centre, such as the RSPCA, for expert advice. They will be happy to help you, even if you have not adopted your pet from their centre.

PET GUIDE

Learn more about other popular pets with these bestselling RSPCA pet guides